A sip of wind

NORA SIMÕES

Picture Show Press

To Baba for blessing me with your love and passion for people, the world, and writing. I will miss you forever.

To Madilyn, Sabrina, and Clark—never ever give up. I love you three with every morsel of my being and with every breath that I breathe.

To Dario for always encouraging, pushing, and supporting me. I love you for sentimental reasons.

POEMS

Resolve

I thought about my mother
today while preparing lentil soup
using a gas stove.

I almost called her
to ask if it was olive
or vegetable oil that went in,
but I took the risk and added olive.

Bread was rising in the oven.
My soup was still in the pot.

I dipped a wooden spoon in,
gave it a stir,
and peered in, waiting
for something to happen.

I covered the pot,
turned up the heat,
and stood back
for the kitchen to explode.

If I were a pig in Brazil

I would have no tongue,
brain, liver, lung, or spleen.

My ears, a severed pile
of chopped cartilage,
would plummet,
along with my tail
and feet, to the center
of a pressure cooker
full of black beans
and bouillon.

My sense of smell
would be stripped,
snout lacerated by the sharp
incision of serrated steel,
hairs scraped like fish scales,
garlic and vinegar shoved
into my nostrils for pickling.

My heart would be
stabbed into a skewer
full of other hearts
being seared in rows,
lined single-fashion

and my stomach would
be ripped out
for the purpose of a
stew meant for slaves.

City of Small Pines

He went to Brazil to find green corn ice cream.
In the stiff airplane seats,
all he could think of were small plastic spoons
and sweet corn, creamed and cooled.

He drank from a bottle of spring water,
gripping the clear cap and peering
out a small, paned window.

On the bus ride to his city,
the hairs on his big toe twitched.
He was happy.
His *tia* greeted him at the station.
There were also twelve cousins, two uncles,
and a bundle of friends from his old high school.

Oi!
      Olá!
            Que saudades!

Before long, his arms were decorated with begonias
and his shoulders with necklaces of braided sugar cane.

He was a man now.
He enjoyed drinking *maté* from a wooden gourd
and sucking *pinhão* from the pit of a leathery shell.
He never added sugar to his tea
and the skin around his eyes had begun to pleat.

This was his first trip back
and he was glad the cold season was beginning
because in his city,
when it became winter, bones froze
and only warm bacon from a popcorn vender

could coat the insides of his cheeks.

When he dropped his luggage in front of the door
where he etched the name of a girl he used to love,
he realized he was home.

Gisele
    e Maurício.

   Te amo.

He remembered the days
of swallowing her saliva,
flicking her tongue with his,
and feeling
for the first time,
       breasts,

a set of breasts
warm and luscious under a blouse
that should have been wine.

He was home
and the cheese was sliced.
The bread was still warm from the baker's,
and the *empadinhas* were rising in the oven.

If he could have drunk the moisture
from the air, he would have,
but he was in Brazil and the only thing
for him to do was swim.

Finished

On the bed he lies
with sheets covering
him waist down and she,
at his side, breasts pressed to him,
arm, naked, on his chest
as they both share the
same breath.

I don't hear the phone

When we're in the shower,
I don't hear the phone ring.

The water falls fast and changes
temperature depending on what the
neighbors are doing.

The towel hangs from a warped
rod on the back of the door.

My green loofah is rich with lather
from liquid soap the scent of
lavender and vanilla.
A drop the size of a pea is enough
to make it last for hours.

The letters on his bar of soap
have been worn down by his
callused fingers, skin ripped off by
the sharp corners of his teeth while
he watches a show that tightens his nerves.

The tub fills so the underside
of our foot arches are covered,
toes warm,
but our ankles shiver.

The hair on his legs looks darker.

His hand slips off my hips,
and I don't hear the phone.

I kiss his lips,
water hitting my ears,
sending us both toward
the crash of ocean.

The beans would tell them

There are garbanzo beans in my sink. They rolled off my cutting board when I tried slicing slivers for a spinach salad with hearts of palm and avocado. They may have danced away when I crushed garlic in my mother's wooden mortar and pestle. Anyone who saw the garbanzo beans would know what land I'm from, that my parents saw wars and widows bellowing atop balconies overlooking the hills of the ancient. They would know I was slapped. I was held at gunpoint by my own kin. They would know because the beans would tell them.

Insolence

I sliced the sausage
with a big knife,
slid them from
the cutting board into
a pot of crackling oil.

Each ringlet popped,
almost jumping out of
the pot and onto
my red toenails.

I covered the pot with
a heavy lid that danced,
steam punching to escape
like a body
scraping the walls of a coffin,
skin wearing thin
like the casing of a meat link
reduced to a thread.

Just Married

We slept in every bed at Ikea,
had their Swedish meatballs for lunch,
and put our hands on all their sheets:
stitched, striped, solid, and satin—
thread counts in the highs and lows,
even pillowcases to match.

There were offices predesigned,
kitchens, dens, and lofts decorated by
a graduate from the Ikea School
of Interior Design.

There were dining tables, small and square
like the person I was becoming,
and chairs, stiff and pressed
like the penis in my husband's pants.

In less than twenty minutes,
during an afternoon of shopping for our new place,
we went from being an interracial couple,
aesthetically uncoordinated,
to a pair of medium-bristled toothbrushes
in front of a foggy mirror.

From here the trees look sexy

The tall one looks
strong and has
many leaves.

The smaller one
is sparse
but has a plump
trunk.
When the wind
blows, its leaves
rustle loud
though there are few.

The trees belong
to my neighbors
whose lights are on.

I can see through
their curtains,

and my husband,
who's sleeping
next to me,

is in the unfortunate
situation not to
have noticed
these trees,
or else he has never
mentioned them.

Perhaps if he *has*
noticed them,
he would be swaying

as the tall tree outside
is swaying—or he
would be fixed
in the soils
reaching underneath
to lift me
like a dancer.

With the grass for a bed

We'd make love like mantes,
you'd be headless,
your penis mechanically
probing without the
need for a brain,
and your body
a buffet for me to feed on.

As spiders, I would be
on top, devouring you
in small crunches until
the last thrust pushes
you into eternal stiffness.
You would surrender
yourself to the clenching
of my jaws or else
shackle me within the ropes
of your webbing.

If you were my drone,
we'd collide in flight,
an embrace propelling
thick liquid inside me
like water from a fire hose,
an explosion leaving your
body lifeless and penis lodged
inside the duct
of a queen adroit enough
to rupture your rifle
without a flicker.

Impotence

He lured her in
with a few short tugs
on a shiny jig,

stuck a gaff through
her ribs to pull her up.

When she struggled,
he cracked her skull
with the heel of his boot,
and measured her
against a thick ruler,

holding her long enough
for the scales to stick
to his hands and the salt
to cover his face,

before throwing
her back in to be
swallowed whole.

Just Factors

Every wedding has a centerpiece.
They want us to take something home
in case they don't.
The napkins are stained with champagne toasts,
the tables engraved with fourteen karats.
This is the beginning.
Of otiose nights,
tobacco kisses.
Of working late at the office,
getting nails primped by a Vietnamese lady
always trying to push a flower.
Only five more dollars.

This is the beginning.
Of fish stirring in an aquarium,
swimming among plastic trees
and fiberglass rocks,
of birds chirping on perches
or branches, just factors,
like the partner in the bed,
stationary and withered
within a universe
not interested in sentiment
or durability.

At the park

Arms flailing, she shouted Arabic words
while her daughter stood stiff
as the pine trees around the lake.

The family at a nearby bench
smoked strawberry tobacco
from a hookah bubbling water,
ate nuts from a bowl made of cedar.

The men played backgammon.
The women prepared coffee,
the handle of the kettle melting
into the barbeque,
thick coffee rolling onto coals.

The fire silenced.
Black dust filled the air
and they choked,
one at a time,
the baby last, a quick choke.

The shouting stopped.

The Sinking

My father tells me he's dying.
My mother's in the bedroom,
asking me to thread needles.

The fog outside melts,
seeps through the cracks
in our ceiling,
and drips into buckets like
rain falling through a sagging roof.

There are noises in the basement.
The dust down there is heavy,
thick,
and pushes up against
the floor we stand on,
through the seams between
each wooden panel that lines our steps.

The dust fills our lungs.

Cigarette smoke fills my father's lungs.
He smokes in the living room,
sitting in a brown couch with an ashtray
on his lap.
   His hand covers mine, a blanket
   over my repining knuckles.

"You will be fine," he says,
"Take care of your mother."

She is still in the bedroom
with the needles.
Soon she will yell at me
for not threading them.

Soon, the dust and fog
will coalesce into mire,
and the three of us will flounder
until we suffocate
from the weight of mud on our chests,
and the only thing binding us
will be the trilogy of our toes meeting
before our eyelids drop like a red,
velvet curtain.

No Sign

I missed my father's burial,
the lowering of his coffin,
the mourning,
and sentience
of running barefoot
toward an ice-cream truck.

At twenty-seven,
running bare hands over
grave markers covered
in pine needles,
nicked palms,
bloody against the thighs of dirty jeans.

There is no sign.

Next to my aunt and uncle,
there's an empty space
where his name should be,
with a picture, an inscription,
and a prayer.

I sit upon the vacuity,
remove my lunch from a slinky bag
with a smiley face on it
and the word "Enjoy".

I'm sitting on a bare plot
eating lunch with my father

or someone.

I pinch a piece of chicken,
a broccoli floweret,

a sliver of boiled cabbage.

There are several stones surrounding me.

It's a hot day.
Torrid.
The grass is cold and a little wet.

There are people
sitting on lawn chairs,
and there are flowers
wrapped in clear plastic
with notes and ribbons.

I didn't bring flowers.

I brought lunch and tennis shoes,
and put an acorn and a coffee bean,
a sugar cube or three,
sesame seeds,
a vile of molasses,
orange blossom water,
and two teaspoons of tobacco
in a small velvet bag with a pull string.

I thrust my chopsticks
into the soil,
a stake to hold the bag down,
so it doesn't get picked up by
wind and ascend into a sky
that won't drop rain
or bullets.

Bleeding of Song

There is a *oud* in my closet.
The belly is large
and the tiles are cracked.

I will play when I am twenty,
I said. I will play it when I am
more than twenty,
when I am a mother,
when I have learned how to work the strings,
when.

A blanket drapes over it,
covers its face.

Two dents adorn its neck
and there are bruises on its collar.

Perhaps I will run my fingers over the bruises,
caress the dents.

There will come a time.
With its belly nestling,
I will hum,
sing while the sallow's leaves kindle
under the moon's dark frame.

Perhaps the flies will sing too
or they will hover
and invite the crows to caw,
their grating cry,
the music's banter,
the suffering of nighttime,
and the bleeding of song.

Corn Husks

She flinched when I put my hand
on her stomach, probably because
it was cold from the saltwater,
from breast-stroking in the turtle's waters.

Due in a few months,
her navel was flat, and I wanted
to rub over it with my index finger,
to feel the sweet reversion
of untouched skin.

The girl inside,
if she looks like her mother,
she'll have long toes
and flared nostrils.
She'll smile at old people
and children, cook tamales
if I come over hungry.
She'll make the *masa*
from scratch, grind the corn
with a grey stone, and fill the husks
before our cheeks even touch.

How I know I'll be a Good Mother *or* A Toad Named Buckley

His belly is red and speckled. At night,
he barks to compete with the sound of tapping

on my keyboard. He jumps high, sticking to
the glass of an aquarium filled with

brown rocks and a hose posed as a waterfall.
That's when I really get to see his belly,

when he's pressed against the inside of misty
glass, barking and begging for a meal.

Sometimes he hides inside a rock. Sometimes
I go in and seek him, dipping my hand in the water

before holding his body on my fingertips. Before
leaving for work this morning, I kissed the glass

and threw a few crickets in to show him what
a good boy he'd been. He jumped onto the glass,

belly exposed and mouth muffled by the gut
of a twitching   cricket.

Zanchin[1]

The hill was steep.
The morning sun
hadn't yet dried the
moisture from the
grass, and my shoes
slipped.

When I closed my
eyes, a butterfly brushed
my ear with its wings.

The dirt smelled a little softer.

I thought I might find
the butterfly to see
what color it was.
Orange maybe,
with black striping.

The air was quiet.

       My ankles were grinning
and my navel waited for a drop of rain.

If I caught the butterfly
and stroked it with my finger,
my finger would be covered
in orange powder.
Could I blow it off like chalk dust?

---

[1] *Zanchin*, or "state of total awareness," is used when training and in combat. *Zanchin* allows the martial artist to be aware of what's around her, to have a sort of sixth sense.

The tree trunks tasted like milk,
      the branches like sugar cane.

The sun spoke in Japanese.

My earlobe touched a falling maple leaf,
      and my body was covered in nectar.

The butterfly landed on the coppery
ends of my hair,
 and fluttered.
      We shared a breath
      and a sip of wind.
It fluttered again,
so we drank the earth,
and became cherry blossoms.

In Vietnam I Would Be Two Rivers

My friend Christina is Vietnamese.
While at her parents house, over a lunch
of *phó* swimming in fish broth and
beef tripe, I learned her real name is
Pham Thanh Truc.

Her family name is *Pham*.
That comes first because it comes
from her father.
Thanh represents her generation,
so her brother, Tom, better known
by his mother and father as *Dat*,
has the same middle name.

According to Christina's mother,
who stands on a stool and hovers over a
frying pan of prawns, *Truc* means wish,
and *Truc* is Christina's given name.

"Christina has been given her wish
because she has a mother so wonderful,"
Mrs. Pham says and then gives a modest chuckle
into her right shoulder.

"If I was born into a Vietnamese family,
what would my name be?" I asked.

"Ha Ha," Christina's mother said and I wasn't
sure if it was another small chuckle or if
she was answering my question.
Over a cup of thick Vietnamese coffee with
condensed milk and two drops of liquid
sugar, Christina tells me that *Ha* means river.

"Does your mom think I should be named
River River?" I asked.

Christina laughed
or maybe
she was calling me by my new name.

ACKNOWLEDGEMENTS

This book wouldn't have been possible without the following:

- Editor and Publisher, Shannon Phillips, for her belief and support in me, her loving spirit, her patient gentility, and her super incredible editing skills.

- Stuart Rosenberg for his belief and support in me, for re-introducing me to writing, inspiring my love for poetry and fiction, and for always being a mentor and friend. Without you, this book wouldn't have been possible.

- Mary Forman, for being my first creative writing instructor, for inviting me to so many workshops and open-mics, and for being a supportive friend and mentor.

- My husband, Dario Simões, for pestering me to publish a chapbook for over 15 years, and for being my #1 fan.

Some of the poems in this book first appeared in the following publications: *A Nation of Long Beach Poets*, *Askew*, *Pearl Literary Magazine*, *Chiron Review*, and *VerdadVerdad*.

ABOUT THE AUTHOR

Nora loves people and all living beings, the way the mind works, emotional complexities, the perfect bite, playing with reckless abandon, butterflies, the garden, deep sea fishing, camping, hiking, shooting paper targets and good ol' fashion competition.

She is a Community College English Instructor who earned her M.F.A. from California State University, Long Beach, and her poetry and book reviews have been featured in *A Nation of Long Beach Poets*, *Askew*, *Pearl Literary Magazine*, *Chiron Review*, *VerdadVerdad*, *Rip Rap*, and *Sole Image*.